CSU Poetry Series LV

For Ann Begler

and in honor of Lewis Mumford (1895-1990)
whose books I carried while writing these poems

Judith Vollmer

The Door Open to the Fire

Cleveland State University Poetry Center

Acknowledgments

Thanks to the editors of the following magazines, where some of the poems have appeared:

Asarte: "The Sound of the Slap," "Tell Me about the Peacocks & Fountains"
The Burning World: "The Stoop Cleaner"
The Illinois Review: "Passing the Clinic in a Small Town"
Ontario Review: "On Reporting the Murder of a Young Prostitute"
Many Mountains Moving: "Asleep at the 2001 Club, Early Seventies"
West Branch: "The Approach"
Witness: "My Sublimation," special issue on American Cities; "Canning Cellar, Early Sixties" and "The Night Trains," special issue on Work in America.

The following poems appeared, often in earlier versions, in the limited edition chapbook *Black Butterfly*, which Mark Doty selected for the 1997 Center for Book Arts Prize, published at the Center, 626 Broadway, New York, NY, in 100 letterpress copies signed by the author: "Saying Good Night to Roses," "My Sublimation," "The Summer Cousins," "The Sound of the Slap," "Passing the Clinic in a Small Town," "Asleep at the 2001 Club, Early Seventies," "Poem at an Unmarked Grave," "Ode to the Black Butterfly," "The Stoop Cleaner," "Tell Me About the Peacocks & Fountains," "Street Poem in April," and "The Night Trains."

"Star Gazing with My Brothers," and "We Built This City" were published in a limited edition anthology in honor of the Fourteenth Anniversary of the Hemingway's Tuesday Night Reading Series in Pittsburgh.

Thanks are also due to the National Endowment for the Arts for a 1993 poetry fellowship which enabled the completion of several of the poems in this book; to the University of Pittsburgh at Greensburg for a Summer Scholarship Grant; and to Blue Mountain Center for a residency in 1995.

ISBN 1-880834-41-3

Library of Congress Catalogue Card Number 98-070394
Published by the Poetry Center at Cleveland State University
1983 East 24th Street, Cleveland Ohio 44115-2440

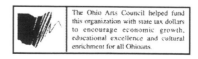

The Ohio Arts Council helped fund this organization with state tax dollars to encourage economic growth, educational excellence and cultural enrichment for all Ohioans.

Contents

III.

IV.

We emerged upon that ugly confusion
of backs of buildings and crazy galleries
and stairs, which always abuts on water,
whether it be river, sea, canal, or ditch:
and were at Pittsburg.

Mile after mile I walked, without
the slightest sense of exertion,
dozing heavily, dreaming constantly.

—Charles Dickens

Saying Good Night to Roses

Surely, after midnight,
they're Persian—*persica*—
molten peaches
lifted from
a lemon-magenta fire.
Fire in my face
when I place them in water,
fire down in the street

in a barrel
where 100 strikers
are warming their hands
against the massive chill
of 2 wealthy men.
"Beep if you support us!"
and I beeped, dead-tired
driving home. I came in
and poured a glass of merlot,

the roses still sleeping
in their crisp paper.
Everybody I love is sleeping,
the kitchen's a cafe:
smoke, mirrors, black & white
tile with hairline cracks.
To read, to sleep, to walk
around the table
dizzy with their scent—

Velvetheads!
I want you for your ideas!
Your brainpetals
revive me just enough to wonder
what my dreams will be like.
The passageway opens
and I wander
in, remain
your modest
beholder,
in love,
good night.

I

My Sublimation

I wasn't talking about the trees,
I was talking about the drive through the Corliss Tunnels
and the dark cinder trail leading into Fairywood
in the West End where under fog that falls
like spoonfuls of gray sorbet
Pittsburgh stands in for Paris, San Francisco,
even a minor, gritty Rome—look at the seven hills,
the parapets & mushroom towers,
the rivers' pewter blades chopping the wharves.
Freud was more than
a little off, none of this is larger than life.
Bridges drip benzene and Neville Island is something you don't
want to look at, well, maybe from the air.

Take the art away from the artist
and we have a crazy person, the great man said.
Take away the gothic Union Trust masterpiece
and you have the Alcoa building & its crenelated aluminum
of the Fifties. The mild narcosis
of the Golden Triangle seen from the air
is our vulva, our hieroglyphic opening
to the nine-mile stream winding its oiled black veins
under our streets.

Do statues really move at night?
Have those who point down at us
from the Carnegie and who lounge on their forearms
along the river merely been visiting all these years?
Whatever's fragrant this evening when we walk back
to our cars & houses is carried on the wind blowing
from the Laurel Mountains.
There's one stand of goldenrod along the fence
at Neville Island. I forgot
the stifling breath goldenrod can fill a room with.

After 235 years you can get a decent cappucino in Pittsburgh.
We don't know yet what this means but we know it's a *lie*
to say art has replaced steel or
that many writers have work. We do know

the categorization of everything has arrived here too.
Your friend shows up at a party wearing
a cocktail dress with a leather jacket
somebody's bound to say, *Where'd she come from?*

It would be cheaper to abandon Pittsburgh than rebuild it,
Frank Lloyd Wright said. Then again
he designed Fallingwater without a decent chair
to sit in. I live inside
this town so this is how I talk.
You can write about rivers all you want
but the truth is
most peole here
have never even touched the water.

On Reporting the Murder of a Young Prostitute

I stood over her,
thought: *Draw me something,*
show me what you look at
when you're dreaming—
cops elbowed past me adjusting lights, tape,
markers. The air was still thick with her
cologne, and her body covered except for her face
& lovely hair, and I was useless.
She made a bargain with herself & somebody
else in an airport motel while
jet trails made their lines above our heads.
I phoned my editor and tried
my slender theories: planned hit
or courier fuckup.
Who was she and what story could I tell,
I was so young myself,
first writing job
in a newsroom high off the street
above the yellow rivers & everything
about the city changing.
One of the last kids
to work the Edison Hotel's mini-
coke & skintrade. Worked
hard. Paid envelopes of cash.
She was 24, a size 4 or 6.
Beautiful nails. Beside her sat
a cheap leather case, like
art students carry.
I believed deBeauvoir:
The worst a woman can do
is to exchange her body for capital.

         **

        As I remember her
she looked like many of my students do now,
dressed for class as for the clubs.
She loved stones as much as they do.
Engagement rings their men

save for. The size and heft of a love.
Delicate enameled friendship
rings from their girlfriends.
Gaudy class rings
paid for by aunts
or godmothers. Yesterday
a student I hardly know
wept in the parking lot:
"I can't remember who all I slept with last night."
She went to a party
of five partners & five rounds.
She remembers that much.
She's 20, pretty, mostly unhappy.
I wonder why she's in school.
I'm tired of chalk outlines,
tired of blind sympathy.
I offer her a sip of my Pepsi
& half of my sandwich.
To her I'm blind.

Asleep at the 2001 Club, Early Seventies

The dead hunting
and the alive, ahunted.
—Frank O'Hara

The boys were in the bathroom doing poppers
& tabbing their scores: six, eight, ten fucks that night
in a modest city far from the Castro or Key West.
Hating disco
I sat out another dance
while everybody else got it on, all body no mind
(my problem, no one else's).
The drag queens were lovely in their dark gloves
& strapless gowns, but I was drowsy
meaning high so I lay down under a long
corner table, first to watch two beautiful kids grind—
but lightly, lightly into each other's crotches
and what joined them till their
cocks strained, sculpted—and I fell into

my persistent dream
of the bacchantes
who in their equal passions for wine & dance
snaked & leapt inside their circle till they lost
consciousness one night in the town square
of Amphissa, city at war with their home
district, Phocis. The old women of Amphissa
stood guard over their dance & their collapse
till dawn, then offered them food & wine
before escorting them out of town.

When I woke up I didn't know
what to do but I tried
to make a painting, a fresco
out back on my garage wall
where the molds are ripe & thick.
I designed it at the last minute after hours
of lying on my couch doing nothing
then executed it quickly, at the last minute,
then finished it with fish & shells
hanging in the market stall
and platters of fruit, bread & cheese
& strong coffee because morning

carries the darkness & bittersweet
resins of the night before.

The bacchantes were neither goddesses nor special,
they were who they were, revelers, 500 B.C.
who wore the skins of leopards to celebrate
their speed & grace. Who loved breaking
the skin of the grape, and dancing & the heavy sleep
that came after. I love them
for their open beauty
and transparent pleasures,
the human being alert to its physical character
without interference.
                                    Where is the red-haired boy?
Gone to Cleveland & the string of fifty lousy jobs.
Now he's buried, ashes flung into the sea.
Where's the black-haired guy who played Strider,
the secret protector of Middle Earth,
who'd straddle a stool at the coffee bar
and then whirl off
like a magnificent feline prince?
Now he's buried, bones quilted to roots & stones.

I didn't see them when they went down. For years
they favored my breakfast table or rode the passenger
seat to the liquor store. For years they talked
while I was talking, or their faces stared
at mine, insomniac. Which is what the dead do.
Do you believe that? I drew on that, I'm sucking
on it now. I could no more
escort them to a safe place
than I can read a topographical map
or cry without making sounds.
We were friends
and held the door open to the fire.

Poem at an Unmarked Grave

Your grave is untouched by flowers
I might have brought.
You left me this fierce love of spaces.
My newest memorial to you
is a meadow garden holding stones
of many shapes: mushroom, serpent,
loaf of bread. You enter through the East
and spiral through it
till you come to two log chairs.
It's stunning
the way wind through the pines
still can't make the sound of your voice.

"Everyplace is like everyplace," you'd laugh
those nights we stayed enchanted
till dawn at your drafting table smoking
and drawing boulevards & libraries.
Your front windows above the shining intersections
were the eyes I used: the body
of Pittsburgh curved under snow,
sculpted finally into our dreams of it, whole,
the public domain of the universities & factories
met the sturdy chimneys & streets of our privacy.
We were twenty and lived inside Emerson's miracle:
a college education is a room with a fire
inside a strange city.

The Sound of the Slap

I've carried the scream
all afternoon in O'Hare.
Maybe I'm the only person
carrying the sound

from the ladies room where I found her
bracing herself against the cold tile wall
hiding from her mother

her mother's voice insistent
calling her for medicine & cleaning
calling her to the white sink

I walked in as the woman with well-dressed hair
& well-fed body pulled her child by the hair
slapped her full across the face then shoved

the medicine stopper into the twisted mouth
while the child screamed and tried to move.
Inside my stall I could hear other women

running water & tearing paper, then clicking out
avoiding the mirrors at the sink
where the woman held on to her child,

now cleaning, now stopping to slap
the red nutmeat of her face.
The skin of my cheeks stings

I'm just one person
but I have a mouth
but I said nothing

My Mother's Wartime Jobs, 1943-45

Her 9 to 5

I filed papers for the rich boys:
orders in, out, number of beams, gears,
parts for bombs built down the river
past the Point. The point was,
nobody here went off to fight. Oh
we kept the war papered & penciled.
I penciled on my seams, drew them up,
ankle to thigh, every morning. I put
my makeup on when I got to the office:
I needed the color and it had to last
till lunch. We went out for cottage cheese
& fruit. The rich boys: _____, _____,
& _____. Why name them? You know
the names: their schools stand, their mills
are renovated malls, their boat clubs
line the river. Their neighborhoods
are the ones people still live in.

Her Plans

My little desk had a rickety typewriter
and the floor was clean black & white
squares. Around this little space
that was mine were new offices
for sales reps for all the steelmakers.
I copied plans, did everything longhand,
then typed & mimeod.
They were all out of Harvard & the Ivy League.
Fresh, & young, I was 19.
I saved for my first trip to New York.
It was two sailors & three girls.
The boys didn't know anything about New York
either. We went with 75 dollars each
and came home with 50.

Working for Miss Marjorie Sterling

She was from Pelham Manor,
New York. She did not marry.
She belonged to the Altruism Club.
They met every week for lunch. We loved it
when she was out. She had bucks
because she rented space to eight men.
She had a nephew with whom she spent Thanksgiving.
She was matriarchal looking: tall, dressed well.
She used to sort of hint about clothes...she called me
Miss Gunia...I had one good dress, black,
long-waisted, very plain, and I wore one
string of large ecru pearls with it.
Every time I wore that dress she would say
"Miss Gunia, that is a lovely dress."
When another firm offered double what I was making
I packed my things to leave.
She didn't wish me luck.

Paycheck

At Dulcey's $29.95 would buy a beautiful dress.
Then shoes and of course everything matched.
As soon as you tried on pumps the salesman
would bring out the bag that matched. And hats
were big. Hats were wonderful. My sister
& I would give our money to Mother
so when we needed something we'd ask.
One day she said, "You're spending your money
and I'm giving you mine." So we started:
that's how I got my silver. That's when
I started buying bonds. And that's how
we got the lot. For 750 dollars.
In October Regis came home.
So I quit. I remember the train ride home
on my last day. Everybody said I was nuts.
I mean the men I worked with, not
the girls. The girls all quit. You just
worked till you married and that was it.

The Shell

I ran into a little trouble there with a Mr.
Brown who was a little Scottish man
who would stand behind me while
I was typing and he put his hands
on my shoulders. "You're such a sweet thing!"
"Please just go away" I wanted to say.
Or he'd wait by the elevator at lunch.
I took the stairs and once he
was waiting in the stairwell. He said,
"I'm going to Florida next week. How
would you like to come along?" "Florida?
In the middle of the War? Why?"
He said "I'd like to show you Florida."
I was still so naive. He was like
a clammy little spider
crawling on—and then he'd wait and walk
me to the train at night. And he
got off at Swissvale and I'd be so relieved.
One night he didn't get off and kept
following me. I just kept changing
blocks, didn't want him to know
where my house was. I just put
on a kind of shell so he couldn't
really get closer. I lost him. I was
faster. He fired me the next Monday.

She Shows Me a Photo

That's the Hotel Henry where I ordered
my first cocktail. I thought Manhattan
sounded so great so that's what I used to have. Ooh
they were bad, too sweet! And that's one of the men.
They were nice young men. A few were married
with maybe a child or two. Some were lawyers.
All of them came from money, and Pittsburgh
was one of the places they hid during the War.
They did menial things like write up orders
just like us. They had to come to work in uniforms
and had to wear their khaki suits. I have to laugh.
Curls were in, you know, and I wore
a bow, or flowers on top of my hair.

They promoted me to Redistribution & Salvage.
I handled detonators for bombs, gauges &
machine tools. Then toward the end of my stay
I became a negotiator. I told the men what to do.
It was all business.

A Reporter Witnesses a Piccolo Mafiosi Breakfast

Eight men in their mid-60s, polo shirts, windbreakers.
Regulars, because I'm the only one staring.
Their table is so close I could borrow their cream
or brush the coat of the oldest one
if he leaned my way.
They place their orders and their voices
hush toward each other. One guy senses me and turns.
I freeze over my pancakes but would like to say
I own the Pacino videos, I enjoy my collection of fine Sicilian literature
and believe in unconditional family loyalty.
It's been my way of life for 40 years.
While they eat they pass the little velvet tray
casually around: rings, a tennis bracelet,
nothing flashy. Some of the men
gracefully help themselves,
others smile and pass.
Their senator is dead. Their children are in college.
Their construction businesses have been legit for 20 years.
Now they're rebuilding the city on stadium concerts & riverboat gambling.
They would like a new governor.
I'm taking it all down: faces, license plates.
But there's no fresh body in the river.
No stories to file until the next big
family funeral
when an out-of-town limo with photogray glass
pulls up, bags lifted out and carried
up to the Hilton's prepared suites,
room service poised, phone
& fax secured, exquisitely secured.

Passing the Clinic in a Small Town

marigold, flower of worry
—Robert Desnos

I don't have to climb those steps
between fists of graffiti
and I don't have to walk through the door
and sit and be interviewed by a fearful woman
who will ask me when
and how did I fail.
The woman climbing now
stood next to me at the light; she must know
every street here the way she maneuvered
the stroller over the curb. So she must know
who works up there and who files her papers in the cabinet
then leads her to the steel table.
One time when
my ovaries like stones were heavy with the chemistry
that multiplied millicell by cell every hour
I laid my body down
and a woman whose face was stone
held my hand. I think she hated her job
but knew how I felt.
I turn the corner
and sudden marigolds
heat the traffic island, another version
of garden, where men and women make their crossings
amid globes of orange fire. The workers seem to float into this morning
while I press my wish for the climbing woman,
that the face she sees
be vacant and spacious. That it leads her
the way sidewalks can,
solid and shaped to her feet
like sandals
worn thin, and smooth.

Canning Cellar, Early Sixties

Only women went down
the stone steps
and opened the cupboard
for the muslin blouses & loose skirts.
Then they weren't women anymore,
braids disappeared into turbans & scarves.
In the hundred twenty degree heat
they bowed their shoulders,
they offered the skin of their fingerprints
to the galvanized tubs & red coils.
The glint of knives over buckets of fruitpeel
was power they sharpened on leather
strops. Wet glass, the knives,
& silver teeth of old women—
They all shined.
They set their jaws
like horses numbed to the bit
and braced their ankles against chairs
braced in dirt. Time was nobody's
when tomatoes were dead ripe
and peaches & pears bruised to the touch
and beans multiplied in twelve rows of bushels.

Scan

Near the heart lies the cupboard
into which I carefully filed the ruined breast of my grandmother
then removed it
& her pale blue jars of threads & buttons

In the belly
the angry letters I stitched to the doorways & mountains of Phu Bai
for the 13 months my brother risked everything

Husks of planter's warts removed without painkiller dot the right heel
Cinder fragments from the bad bike accident the left

Lost constellations inside my uterus still glow
for the tissues torn out
My spirit swims and flies there alongside

the pulsing dome of my mother's lost ovary
her mother's 10 pregnancies & 10 homebed deliveries

Veils of my father's insomnia wrap the skull's frontal
interiors so that dreaming wide-awake comes naturally

The hairline crack at the base of the spine
from the summer party I slid, stoned, down a dozen steps

curls like a serpent of wandering intent
its fire another tongue of irretrievable speech

Everywhere the microscopic lines
left by skin on skin, the oceanic & moraine-
kissed traces of lovers

Under the right ribcage are the wild red foxes
I found in a beautiful dream
In bluegray mist where they run
it's always morning, when breathing is easiest

and I awaken
refreshed, restored to this body
this house I carry alone

Street Poem in April

I was just talking to her voicemail,
that's how much I missed her.
It was a high windy Tuesday, cold
so her eyes would be tearing
and she'd be heading for the parking garage
and her ankles would be stiff
and her left arm tight from the briefcase
full of legal papers full of unsettled
fears & lost happinesses. I would have liked,
a few hours later, to have watched her tighten
the laces of her boots and walk into the pink
evening with me because it was an ordinary
evening but there were 700 miles & three
weeks between us; we couldn't have named
where the passages of distance were
except by color: she'd have known exactly
what I meant because it was spring when
colors are most intense and everything the trees
are doing happens fast like the change of light
on, say, an open-air phonestand.
First it's silver & stainless steel, then it's silvery
with green & gray rectangles which are really
shadows of buildings at my back. Then the shapes
of trees in the small concrete islands sway just
enough to enter the frame of the phonestand's
mirror. I see my reflection carries my tenderness for her
even at this distance and I feel my fingers
on the wire in a kind of offering of connection
call it a cord or signal, she'd understand
because of the color of my skin, a little pink
from the sun, a little bronze against the washed
black street the city workers washed this morning
because it's Tuesday and there are blossoms.

II

Ode to the Black Butterfly

I hope the dark creature
whose wings bear triangular fans
of orange satin & Neruda's blue *live metal*
will approach the twisted apple tree
whose fruit I've let drop and rot this summer
for the hungry birds. It's nearly five and every afternoon this week
she's come, alone, or trailing 3 or 4 smaller others
in the fluttering dance they make through the heat
toward sweetness & color. The little ones suck at the red impatiens
or circle the tall dark fronds of the lilies
to dip for the nectar even as the blossoms curl
& dry into petal funnels & closed cones.
But this one, can I call her mine? lands just a few feet
away from where I'm reading in the corner of the yard
where no one can see me though I'm less than 30 feet
from Milton Avenue & its pre-rush-hour river of cars. I have wanted to be
a tambourine player in the service of Aphrodite. Is that so strange?
Once, the creature rested on my wrist
the way damselflies sometimes do up at Blue Mountain
and once she rested at the edge of the birdbath, then swayed
off again for more sugar. Right now, as if she's wobbly with excitement
or desire, she lands, half-folds her wings and walks
over to the single yellow apple she's chosen from some impossible
aerial path. She walks so slowly I think
she'll change her mind
and take off again, then climbs up onto it and walks down inside
a narrow ditch of brown rot and rests her wings while she feeds.
I feel cooled inside her darkness, her flight
under the arcs of the great bridges and into
our woods on her way across the city to here.
What can I make? What can I save?
This beauty can't save me
but she has the power to stop time this afternoon
in the August drought while I wonder
how far she's traveled; last night,
did she skim over the surface of the river lightly, so
lightly then touch down, did she bathe
a millimeter of wing tip on the silver water?

The Night Trains

I stood and I watched
the destruction of the lovely Arcade,
a poor woman's *Milano* where ladies bought hats
& fancy boxes to keep them in. Then the tearing
down of the houses of the poor,
whole neighborhoods slid under the crust of our earth
where barrels & trunks from the old
countries rot inside the clay. We are trying to make

the haulaway go more quickly now, take the husks
& boxes of pipe, tubing, bodies of furnaces, warehouses
of loose rust and load them. We are trying to bury
all of it, we are trying to do what the old *studdabubbas*
hissed at us to do: Clean up after yourself before
someone else has to. But there's so much
mold & rust, I want to forget, late at night
in the minutes I try to save for rest

until I hear the trains coming through
carrying their garbage from New Jersey,
cars full of gauze & blood & human hair, the teeth
& dull fur of the test animals.
How much have you lost?
Have you listened in happiness for a train,
near your hour of sleep, listened for its generous
throat to fill the city air
with its sweet burnt sugar & smoke? I
hear too many trains
after the 1:30 and before the 6.

I think about some lonely giant woman
having to clean up all the mess, she has to shovel
it into something, scrape everything into a bucket
tipped on its side, while sludge & girders roll
out again. She fills & fills her bucket, scrapes
the railyards & asphalt to ebony.
Still there is plenty
for the halls of the underground
city & its hurtful shine.

What She Didn't Tell Him

A few days later, after blood
& the tearing out,
after the thumbnail embryo
had been sent on its journey
through the great waterworks
of our wastes & tender freedoms,
she remembered one afternoon
among the long days waiting
in fear, how snow fell
onto the trees, pressed
intricate lines into their
wet branches, and something,
call it joy, caught her
in happiness so pungent
she laughed, her hair glossy,
her fingers light
over the paperwork as she
thought of nothing
at all but watched snow
and felt a swift
fluttering inside her
when she least expected
lightness.

Knowing That You Know Things

From my porch, I sweeten my evening
by gazing up into the filigreed locust.
And now I know
Pennsylvania smartweed doesn't smart
when you bite into it. Its dark pink
border joins *Diodia*, or buttonweed—Greek
for *thoroughfare*—along the sidewalk to the alley.

Spread enough needlegrass on the floor,
walk into the house and see it shine.
Dream the dream about Dick Hugo again
at the country fair on the dusty road
where he bought you a little clay hash pipe.
Try to avoid the deadly sins: chastity, want of money,
not writing stuff down,
knowing that you know things—

I started this the day I saw an old woman
gathering chicory—ragged sailors—
on the thruway ramp. We're inside a city
7 hours from the Atlantic Ocean
but those sailors held their blue against her
gray hair, our gray sky. I was driving, I don't think
she sensed me there slowing down.
She kept gathering. Later I cut some
of the flowers and thought of baking the roots
for coffee but they were dank & tough.
I took some prunella, carpenter weed
& the daisy fleabane
& broomsedge for the ancient housewives—
"Sweep your floor and your feet feel better."—

Nimble Will, the drop-seed,
frames the backyard fence
where the Rhus sumac
stand with their whips & fans.
Once in a while
I take a knife to them
letting the strongest stand.
It's taken me years to love them.

We Built This City

on violins & accordions,
eighteen-wheelers
& the Firing Squad of Henry Clay Frick.
Blood-stained panties
buried in landfills,
sweet & harmless drunks, too many to count.
The ideas if not the realities
of Pericles.
Coalbuckets, workbuckets, stolen goods.
Children dead because they were children.
Lost women.
Cocktail napkins covered with hieroglyphic
laments & secrets of the Universe.
Powdered human bonemass in vials
locked inside the biotechnology labs.
Cock rock, dyke rock,
proto-grunge & funk.
Jazz. Too many evolutions to count.
A stolen Picasso lithograph
bearing lyrics composed millennia ago.
Sleeping bags & Coleman lanterns.
Dogs, too many to count,
tongues congealed in the 110 degree heat.
Veils on veils of strontium & benzene.
Christmas shoppers wading through snowdrifts,
                    Smithfield Street, 10 p.m.
Tunnel light, color of limestone.
Ingots, too many to count.
The *idea* of the Left Bank.
The idea of city.
Windows, 6 p.m., sunstruck, gray mabé pearls.
Timberlands, Wolverines, Sears Steeltoes
                    balancing on scaffolding & airspace.
Rented tuxes, colors too many to name. Pussies wet & wet.
Kohl sticks worn down to nubs.
Application of the theory Marco Polo used to change Venice:
                    Bring in news from the Outside.
Sidewalk gardens of eggplants & basil.
Flutes.

Tunnels like flutes.
The last of the Section Eight Urban Redevelopment Money.
The last of the UDAG Grants.
The last of the Nelson Rockefeller Republicans.
The Democratic Machine that ruled for a century.
The idea of city.
The dream
            of what *polis* might mean.
The giant fusilli & ziti
of sewerpipes, too many to count.
The significance of the IRON OVER WATER
                                    hexagram of the I Ching.
Oak office desks polished with lemon oil.
Rice cakes, rice paper, thin mats & bells.
A bridge half woman, half dragonfly.
Sharpened yellow pencils & fragrant grey lead.
Jaroslav Seifert's "Song of the Sweepings."

The Summer Cousins

For their dark lipsticks arranged in a golden fan,
for their strong radios primed with fat batteries
& the Chicago station doing blues all afternoon
& for their eyelet underthings
dampened & rolled in the willow basket
because ironing transported those girls—
& me, initiate & pet—
from the family's tight fist
downstairs in the steamy cube of kitchen
& the spoiled uncles' *na zdrowie's*
& the cranky aunts' *zostancie z Bogem's!*
A hot steam iron could point a collar & pout a sleeve
or smoothe a bodice crisp with appliqué.
My cousins' naked meditation over the white board
was so full of their heat
even the steel window screens & fanblades
gave light in the dim half hours
just before Saturday night.
The younger one brought me cold green
bottles of ginger ale and smirked she had gone
all the way more than once.
The older sat with me over embroidery
placing my fingers on the French knot
till I felt how it was made.
No books in that house, no talk of college.
But permission to brood and read
& pause while reading my *Great Expectations*
& my *Far From the Madding Crowd*
and look up into their preparations for the world.
What was it out there in the dark
I wanted? Boys feared me and girls broke my heart.
I think that summer I made my first decision:
to pay attention, under the spell
of taffeta, words to a song and, best,
the sweet drug of my cousins' secrets
on the dressing table
of cigarettes & fast handwriting in open diaries
& twenty five tiny glass bottles of scent.

My Great Aunt Writes from the New Poland, Early Seventies

Kohana Judita/Dearest Judith:

In Zakopane they're selling
souvenirs for half price.
They made too many.
Our neighbor has a car now,
he was given it so
he can spy on everyone better.
Here the rains fall day by day, a day
or two of sunshine and then again rain.
The little bridge over the brook is useless
because the water is so high.
The belt for your blouse was left here—
too bad because the embroidery
is of the same colors.
And a little notebook
with your handwriting in it.
It must have fallen behind the bench
and I do not know how
to send it. Here we had another
mild winter. I didn't have to sweep
any snow, only move more straw in.
I was sick. My leg
was very bad
but I'm beginning to walk with a cane.
But I'm not much better. For the dollars,
for the pretty pictures, I sincerely
thank you. Everyone was so
delighted they took
them all from me. And what a wet
summer! Cucumbers, tomatoes, & so
many apples! If you were only closer
I'd bring you a big sack!
This year we had a big celebration, the 25th
anniversary of the priest's ordination.
It was in Kroscienko, the bishop was here.
Anton continues his meetings but
is followed everywhere.
And at Marisha's
there's a little news. Antek has a job

in Krosno. He took me into town.
It was so pretty I wanted to leave my eyes there!
This year there was a great
number of visitors from America
on a vacation but none of them
knew you. I kiss you all around.

Aniela Lorens, Rzeszow

Reading My Lost Polish Diary

for Patricia Dobler

Now I can see
she thought, at 20,
she knew everything.
And she did, in the brilliant
yet momentary way
we're perfectly alive
inside nothing but our freedom
to look and to see:
She visits the ancestral farm
& old women whose sausage legs
match her grandmother's.
She admires her own
darkening olive skin,
color of the farm's earth.
She loves the pure politics
of being a good listener
but has no language
to tell her cousins of the fire
inside her antiwar & women's
symbols, her only adornments.
She pays attention
when the cousins stare
and talk about her
and then return
to their bushels of potatoes & beets.

"My cousins not yet 40, black teeth in their mouths.
Aunt Aniela runs across the log bridge like a girl.
This is a smaller Pennsylvania
rolling through my head. Long kilometers of orange
roofs & hand-pushed plows. Bright-stockinged children.
I love the thimble-sized glasses of raspberry vodka.
The red poppies distinguish the weeds.
My cousins the glass worker & the priest
say Solidarity *will give them the freedom*
to buy land and plant rye. Munya, their cow,
sleeps in Aniela's cabin. Both rooms have dirt floors
& straw stacked two bales high against the walls.
My aunt told me this morning (the priest translating)
I don't know what work is

because my hands are too white.
And I will never learn anything from politics.
And my town is only as good as the people who take care of it.
What's she telling me? Tonight we're going to a wedding
out in the country. To dance with the bride you have to
throw a silver coin hard enough to crack a plate.
They stack the plates high as a table!
They spread sawdust for a faster floor
and the men smash their coins down.
And sometimes a bride will faint.
She has to dance seven, eight hours,
as long as the coins flash."

Now I dream I follow her
inside the arches of Krakow
to wander the arcades.
What am I supposed to tell her?
You can't live on love
& books; someday you'll want
to run away from your life
because making a living
takes too much? I follow
her, sit down and wait.
A box of cartridges for my
old blue fountain pen
sits on the cafe table.
I have nothing to tell her.
What I know now
& didn't then
is all hers. The shops
are dark & cool. I'm going
to buy a carved box & a table cloth
stenciled with red & yellow birds.
The air I'm breathing
floats in from Aniela's village.
By now, late afternoon,
she's sleeping. Everything
she's taught me
has entered my hand
and moves
on this open page.

Ode to Lynyrd Skynyrd

"Friday afternoon always feels sad," Drew says as he & Jen walk me to my
office. They have to work all weekend waiting tables. Dave is leaning
in my doorway, too bored to come in, too pissed not to; he says
I'm trying to make him sound like Norman Dubie, C.D. Wright, or James
Wright. I start packing my papers & gradebook for my weekend.
I just want to read a good poem, I want to say.
He's in new leather head to toe but the t-shirt
has to be 20 years old, maybe an uncle's, or his dad's.
"They're touring," he says. "I know," I say. I don't
say the night their plane went down
I cried, and my friends were gently amused
I'd love a redneck band from Alabama. We hated
the South. We just hated it.
                    Dave's been writing since
high school and I can feel how he wants to be.
I tell him about time and how that's
what being in school gives you. Reading & poems.
I tell him about Parra's great ode the size of the entire
history of his beloved Chile, where "the teachers"
want us to learn the universal law of gravity,
want us to figure how long it would take a train
to reach the moon, etc., etc. I want to make him laugh.
                    Dave's last words: "Anybody ever tell you
you look like Lou Reed?"
                    Later I see him get into his van
with a loud woman & four kids in the back
& headed for one of his two jobs at the mall.
It takes 50 years to grow up in this town, it takes
every drop of sweetness in every genetic cocktail to break
our regional disease
the *why try, why try,*
this in-the-drinking-water
I could do it if I wanted, but...
Don't tell us who we are.
We don't need you, we don't.
We are so far out in the provinces
no postage stamp will memorialize us
though we repair & rebuild our 800 steel bridges
and are home to more deciduous trees than any

other city in the nation. Though we consume
more coffee than any city in the world—check it out:
New England Journal of Health, January, 1993.
When steel left, we built labs.
We replace hearts & livers.
We can't do lungs yet. We bless our oaths
in three rivers at once.
There is an "h" at the end of *Pittsburgh*.
Our version of "Free Bird" always
gets caught in our throats.

III

Self Portrait with Notebook

> *It was exile from domesticity*
> *that produced my poems.*
> —Stevie Smith

I'm so menstrual I'm pathetic, though not too far gone, really,
bathed, collapsed on the couch, the cotton string delicate as
calligraphy curled on my thigh.

*

The moon is big, round & red tonight.
The red bird has whistled every morning all Spring.
Now I have all those notes to sing.

*

Crepe skin, they call this: spidery lines in my wrist.
Turkey neck, they'll say. I have the Slavic chin, and, well,
my neck begins to loosen its taut sleeve. "Honey," my mother
tells me, "wear your pearls while your neck is still good."
That is why
              this morning I committed to memory
              Sylvia Fanaro's poem:

> *I hope to become*
> *a very nice old lady*
> *who will still enjoy*
> *the pleasures of the big city:*
> *speeding around in*
> *my old car,*
> *in the eternal search for*
> *time, money, and love.*

*

My soul brother, recounting a marvelous night, bragged,
"My dear, we did enough fucking
to scrub a floor."

*

To paraphrase Jack Nicholson:
Kiss a tit—*X-rated!*,
but cut it off—*PG 13,*

is another way of saying
the erotic is obsessive & lost
in America,
always eating and being eaten.

*

The more you consume
the more you are consumed.
      I had to forget
the black lace sandals,
the imported cigarettes,
the first edition H.D.
But I bought the fancy pen
that day I pretended I was rich,
fresh from a hotel shower & double espresso
strong enough to wake a horse.
I knew my limit
but ignored it, stunning myself
with how it feels
to be held up inside the material.

*

When the ancients said, dumbstruck:
She bleeds but doesn't die!
they weren't wearing masks.

*

The closest I'd ever come
to a religious conversion
would be to try writing fiction.
Meanwhile, I'm meditating on DiPrima's
"Notes on the Art of Memory
     (for Thelonius Monk)":

   The stars are a memory system
    for thru them

we remember our origin
Our home is behind the sun
or a divine wind

    that fills us
    makes us think so.

*

It's been a long time since I downsized Mao's "Women hold up half the sky"
to my grandmother's wiser Polish saying: "Women hold up
three corners of the house."
Old woman, resting,
read the papers, *Gwizda Pologna/Star of Poland*
and *Jaskolka/The Swallow*
inside the belly of her house,
a bird whose wings
held her
in a fragrance of smoke
& packed earth.

*

Who'd play me in a movie?
    Glenda Jackson and/or Neil Young.
I revere the paleotechnologies: letter & phone.
I believe in death, copulation, & birth.
I believe in the grand gesture,
the double dozen of carnations
tinted aqua & cerise,
two in the buttonhole,
the rest on the kitchen table
in a clean glass vase.
The bedsheets opened like a book,
the long book we open and open.

Eating Reagan

I got it
late, after the Oklahoma City bombing,
while counting the dots
on the *Wall Street Journal* map
marking Klan*Klan*Skinhead*Skinhead
outposts all over
my home state Pennsylvania
right above the Mason Dixon Line
right where the dots have been
all my life, down
past Uniontown &
the Maple Sugar Festival
in Meyersdale, down
near Old Route 40
where the dark mallow flowers
line the bike trail you can ride
all the way to D.C.
to Jefferson's cloud-white marble.

Once, when I woke to my first
schoolyear, when I watched
the black, white & red America
and he came on selling soap
& his own Death Valley face,
I was excited with our new TV
& my first pair of eyeglasses,
paying such close attention—
smart reader, neat handwriter—
to a salesman who would be President
and I remember the handmade models
my fifth grade class was so proud of—
Capitol, Parthenon, the old
Greek oath we memorized:
to be good citizens
"together with the help of all, or,
if not, single-handed."

Later, in a barbaric school
I visited in the 80s

State Troopers were called out
to round up, to bring in,
& to end, once & for all,
the annual rite of cutting classes
on Senior Recognition Day:
the evil almost-graduates
were marched back into the assembly room
& up onto the stage
before the sweaty face of the principal,
and the younger kids were marched in
past the gray guns & leather chinstraps
and seated, alphabetically,
to witness the example.

That was when I met
David Kalada
whose beautiful poem "Old Pond"
still graces my desk.
He got locked
in a refrigerator one summer day
with his sister,
he made it, she didn't,
he wouldn't talk all fall,
a bad teacher
held him back a year,
put him in LD.
But he'd write.
The minute I walked in and started reading
my "poem of the day"
he'd write. I'd watch
his hand move back & forth
inside his hard blue notebook.
He & his friends wrote a letter
about the school food.
Ketchup was a vegetable,
hotdogs were entrees,
lunchtables were checkpoints.
They started showing me around.
Sex was contraband you could get

behind the maintenance building.
A baby could be like a trophy
or a *fuck you*— if you had one
during your senior year.

They were pretty good cynics.
A few were natural writers.
On the playground making poems
& drawings, we were so tiny
gazing up at the sky
and back toward the main entrance.
I told myself the world would be ours
because of *who we were*. I forgot
we make the republic
a few images & deeds at a time.
And nobody
including me
told those kids
their President was wrong.

Counting the dots I realized
Nixon was a dot.
Reagan was a dot.
I had eaten Reagan
like a dot
of blotter acid,
he was tough, pickled & shriveled,
the brain scar tissue &
media blockout
made him grainy
like old beef jerky.
Like one of the dolls from carney nights
when we were children,
the leathery ones we wasted quarters on
to try and win to scare our friends.
I swallowed him,
I absorbed him.
How were we to know he'd fool us?
He felt like nothing going down.

Poem on the Summer Solstice

A new fawn
is resting in the long grasses
beside the lake. Since noon
she's risen twice to turn
on her wobbly legs
and settle back down.
Her tall ears
make their adjustments
to my page-turning sounds,
and when she turns her head
to lick her shoulder
one black eye
looks over at me
while her long tongue moves
between sunlight & the thin
green blades. I have enough
happiness to last all summer.
Last week I dreamed I breathed
my heart out of my own body
and removed from it an inchlong
triangle of scratched brown glass.
I placed the shard on a broad leaf
and floated it off across the lake
over where dark green water
meets silt under the pines.

Now two flickers enter my two o'clock
and tap away.
The pure black & white of them
clears my head. What have I been
worrying about?
Now the tiny marsh between me
& the fawn wakes up too
with mosquitoes & black flies
preparing their phalanxes.
Behind me in the chive flowers
bees & monarchs have been laboring since dawn.
Next week I'll turn 44

inside the tender
heart of middle age.
Heart, you're tough.
You're sharp brown honey.

The Ecology of Baseball

I personally know
at least three women who can throw the fastball.
Everybody knows
good women runners
& 20/20 vision outfielders.
Believe me,
I know women who can hit.

*

Live on cable,
thrilled inside her first triple
against a male pitcher,
the rookie picked herself up after the slide,
forgot herself
and hugged the third base coach.
"That kind of friendly shit has to go," one reporter, off-camera, said.
And the chattering—"It takes them 15 minutes to finish
congratulating each other in the outfield," their coach complained.
But he sounded happy: "Women want it more
than men, they want to get up and start playing
early in the morning and just
keep playing."

*

The past is alive here in the dirt
under square glass boxes at the feet of Clemente.
Our public relic
is the dirt he played on
behind the color barrier
he looked & laughed at.
Children pause to be photographed
under his hands
and hang onto his outstretched fingers.

*

The summer of the Last Big Strike

we took the (scab) replacements,
we wanted to fan ourselves
with playbooks sweet with new ink.
Hope for our city rested
on a 47-mile-per-hour knuckleball
or, ideally,

extra innings & long night games
where the women dress
in bright lipstick & flowered skirts
and the men chill out
and stuff their kids
with the healthy junk food.
And where lovers like the game to last,
a good slow fuck
slow enough to slow
our hard working lives down.

Afterward when we file out
under sky black & silver with stars
we out-swarm the traffic of insects
thickening around banks of lights.
Web of life, web of death,
now the hungry
nighthawks glide in to feast.
All theirs, the shiny bowl & crusted seats.
They swerve into every concentric aisle of air,
driven into it, the cleaning, the clean sweep.

Star Gazing with My Brothers

I have to walk through the darkness to get to them,
down through the cellar then up through the little greenhouse
our father built instead of a bomb shelter in 1960—
I step out onto the patio where they're taking turns at the big black scope,
and another of Jupiter's moons glides out from behind that gigantic
planet of emotions. Rege says we're standing under The Summer Triangle:
there's Albireo, the Double Star. The colors—how can clear fire have color?—
drug me, my father is on his chair murmuring about the War in the Pacific
again: "The Equator was one big centrifugal force, coconuts were falling,
trees were swaying, Manos Island was the most beautiful place
but everyone was lonely." He laughs. Stars are in motion around
his body. I have to turn my back on him to look
into the dark tunnel that leads upward. Saturn's rings slant,
oily dust, here comes the white crystal of Jupiter's hidden fourth moon.

Out here the zinnias touch my right shoulder. This one is black velvet,
this afternoon it was dark red, and these graywhite ones are pink
in daylight. My black sandals are black, my mother's voice is silver
falling down from the kitchen window
where she's wrapping food in foil for her shut-in neighbors
and she's delirious to have all her children here.
I ask Bob where Cassiopeia is and Rege answers. His son Paul
calls me over to get a look at M2 awash with studded
veils of stars on stars. He is so shy & beautiful I want to dance.
Now my brothers are assuring me
there is life as we know it in all the distant places.
Our mother the genius eavesdropper calls down, "Of course,
remember Copernicus."
Here is one of the centers of my world, so momentary
I wonder if it's even a system. A sister might mean anything
to her dreamers-for-brothers. I wish for *friend for life*. How easy
that feels, how fragile here at our childhood home
where every fir tree in the yard was once a tiny Christmas tree,
where the oldest dog is buried,
where I stand with my brothers, we have always been three.

Someone Is Waiting for Zekria

—after John F. Burns of the <u>New York Times,</u> and his early
& powerful coverage of the human face of the war in Bosnia

I've tried to be a good niece,
keep his house, do his shirts, meet him
here for our little talks.
Sit with me, this is his table.
It's ceasefire, real or not, so he'll be walking
Marshall Tito Street in his clean white shirt.
It's a citizen's duty.
Wait with me. We have coffee
& plates of jam made of roses.
Some are eating grass & dogs.
He'll be here in five minutes. He usually
waves at the gunners—
I keep his black shoes polished, he says
they're shiny eyes
seeing everything and being seen.
He just likes to walk
and wave his bottle at gunners
& point his ivory handled umbrella.
We have sold most of our fine things.

We're looking for something to eat.
When he was a child of nine
in April, '45, our city still closed off
by Germans, he'd run into the park
to watch American planes drop supplies
of egg, powdered milk & shoes by parachute.
He called them Truman's eggs.
There are no parachutes now.

We still have something to drink.
Enjoy our jam made of roses.
See my lace handkerchief?
This is part of my duty:
I dress in the morning and walk,
and stop here for coffee & a smoke.

Sometimes I make little notes.
What falls from the sky?
Rain, bombs, glass.
Our city of no glass for windows
lets us look inside to another city.
This time it doesn't belong to anybody.
Our city of weeds promises us this.
Our dead call us to the table
and we join them.

The Stoop Cleaner

She is kneeling on the top step
in veils of fog & icy wind.
Sparks jump from the forward & back push
of her wire brush & hand.
Clouds lift from her bucket
of hot water & vinegar.
Now she moves down
to the second, now the third
step, her arm the only motion
in the street. Two black birds
call out from their sauna inside her
chimney's column of opalescent smoke.
Here I come
up the alley toward her clouds.
When steam turns to ice on her eyeglasses
her quick stop to clear them
reveals the cracked leather of her hand.
Her arms move forward & back,
her feet brace themselves against the edge of curb.
The woman is a black ant in a wool sweater
kneeling on wet cement
now rinsing, now presenting her work
to the birds, the sky, the swath of quiet alley.
It is 7 a.m., twenty five degrees.

It is any & every day
in every season
and when the rinsing frees
all three steps
of hair & footprints
everything washes down
down over the curb and into the street.
Everything blends with the lines of dirt,
the syringes & pulverized needles,
lumps of paper & torn tickets.
Smashed cans, bits of condom,
illegible labels & lost notes.
Here I come up the alley

past the catalogue that washes its way
downhill to the river.
Now she lays down salt
and the weight of her devotion
moves down from her shoulders
into her palms and is released
through her fingers. Salt
turns ice to dissolving lace,
burns it away
off the edges of stone.
I enter her world of devotion
carrying my newspaper & bag of books.
I am not the granddaughter
she adored for half her long life.

She recognizes the rhythm of my walking,
and my high forehead & pronounced chin
match hers bone for stubborn bone.
When she stands up
and looks into my eyes
I feel the alley behind us
stretching itself down to the river.
I feel the river
pulse in its silver mercury
& its sideways stopped-down
shifts downstream.
The skyline in her eyeglasses
disappears behind wind & ice, then reappears
as a slice of glass & bright steel.
I am the granddaughter she adored
half of her long life
and now I stand
on a hillside
curved to the rib-
bones of giant creatures
underground a million years.

Her time here
is finite. But in the fine

calibrations of morning light & wind
I reach a hand to her
shoulder and face.
She is mine, warm, nearly
disappeared.

The Approach

It's May it's Spring it's not going to snow anymore but my nerves
are shot and there are 32 ways to town but I've taken the wrong one

so I'm gridlocked, mid-tunnel, no book, tape, radio reception.
I've been taking the sedatives the dead aunts used: chamomile & catnip,

glass of bitters w/magnesium every evening after dinner—
Can I breathe in here? Mother, can you hear me? Her voice:

*I took you down to the city to buy a party dress. You took your little blue
purse & folded dollar.* I am going to meditate on the immanence

of approach: ahead is a marvelous container, I will dip down
into it and examine the treasures

because I'm alive in the time of great cities. *I took you down,
we took it slow through the tunnel because grooves in the lanes*

made it tough to drive. Smoke & grit are glazing my windshield.
I crawled on my knees holding her hand Good Friday all the way

up to the altar. I did it for the straw basket of candy, the sugar
drug my stomach craved. I did it for the incense and I did it

for nothing because I was told to and to not do it
would make me feel sad in her disappointment. *We saw the city*

*above the yellow rivers behind her grey veils, behind a giant
black cloudful of clouds.* Love is a tunnel on the way home.

The immanence of love is waiting for me in a fragrant
apartment, windows open, wine poured & breathing.

I want to get there and have him
peel my blouse away from my skin. I'm disguised as a working

woman trapped in a dirty tunnel but I'm really about to
divide the cloud cover and reveal another approach:

we find ourselves standing before a great oak door. We know
there's an ocean on the other side, we can hear & smell it.

I can't hear myself think, the drone & stalling grind in their inch-
by-inch forward motion. The walls are slimy & damp with smeared

diesel fuel: the graffiti of pollution. Bumper sticker ahead of me—
YOU CAN'T RAPE A .38. I feel the fear. Gunman three cars up

gets hot, starts blowing people away with nowhere to run.
Last month when a bus exploded in here people—lawyers, nurses

pensioners, students, all helped each other off and led one another
through the darkness. Those simple acts of kindness made

the six o'clock, interview after interview. *She took me by the arm,
my glasses were broken and I couldn't see. He gave me his jacket*

mine had blood all over it. Mother, the first time I ever
made love, your body, a startled white bird, flew out of mine.

You saw yourself flying! You saw the room! bed! your lover's arms & mouth!
No, I saw you there in the room, a white bird saying goodbye.

Mother, why is it every time we talk about
whether our dead know how much we think & talk about them

we decide they don't? *Child, nothing will happen to you
till the day you die.* No. Stop repeating the words of *your* mother.

I know you will live to be very old. But Mother why
are you being peeled from me, from Earth? There's light

behind me. Ahead the city will be dark and dressed
in its white & golden windows & lamps.

I can feel the arms of my mother. And I feel the body
of my own life saying go ahead, you're moving
whether you know it or not.

Tell Me About the Peacocks & Fountains

I put the Dante away, the poem
was beautiful, but the critic's
intrusion on the text made me dizzy.
I had to see him:
the one in the tight chinos
had to see his drumset
his double martini glasses
his bar with the translucent lights
had to see him
turning down his sheets
me in them
had to see his neon condoms
him sliding one on
so I reached for the street
the curb the car door and took the back streets
where tiny houses were so lit up:
I was driving down an aisle
wet as black enamel
up his sidewalk to his door
& goldfish in their shallow china bowl
like Mary McCarthy's fish in Venice
(they were languid but still alive)
He was brooding but drew me to him
leg slung over a wide red chair
pulled me onto his lap
and I was widening
into his open shirt
He told me again
Here we are among the peacocks & fountains

Small cats watched from their intaglio pillows
It was years ago in the poise
of his lightly tanned shoulders
& my dark rose tunic
& how he unfastened it
when I asked him to

IV

Poem Written While Thinking of James Wright
On a Rainy Afternoon

James Wright, dead 15 years,
I stood in the shallows of the Adriatic
and trailed my hands in the aqua waters.
Every morning I inspected the fishing boats
at the red & blue docks, then undressed in the bright
cabana along the walk trimmed with pink & white
stones from the sea. The inn I found
faced the water and I slept peacefully in
Fano, where you were so in love.
Honoring us Americans our host
cooked hotdogs & baked beans for our farewell
though we were only a few steps
from the boats & *frutta di mare.*
I cleaned my plate.
I washed the dinner down
with a good thin red
and went walking.
I didn't think of home once

till I saw the girl
riding the handlebars of a bike
pedaled by a grandmother
who had your face.
The girl was an elf with olive skin
against black wings of hair.
She stared out to sea, then back,
perched on the silver bars.
The old one had your face
and I thought of the book,
the saddest one you soaked in death
& alcohol & Minneapolis
street people worse off than you were.
The girl had your wild spirit & the distances
you traveled beyond that book
maybe because of a few charms you saved, like the one
where you try to blossom yourself
beside a lost man in a boat.
You try to comfort him and fail.
But later you touch and speak

to the smallest creatures and become radiant.
I've carried the old woman & her girl

because, once, when I needed a healing place
they came back to me. In another sea town
I used to sit beside a poor grotto.
I studied its chipped *putti* Owl & its Pan
with crooked pipe-stems.
I was afraid of dying without children
or with them. Afraid was all I was
till the old one & her girl came.
I watched the grotto into the night
after its red & yellow lights flicked on
& the carp slid under the coral to sleep.
I promised to stop feeling sorry for myself.

I don't know what the children saw at Lourdes
or what your hobos saw under the bridges of the Ohio.
Maybe a lost woman who takes the form of a tree.
Or a tree whose windy motions
rock a man & a woman into a trance.

The old one pedals her precious cargo in the rain.

River

—after Robert Desnos

The stones under the water told the fountain:
"Glisten for us."

The fountain told the hilltops:
"You shape the waterways."

The hilltops told the skyscrapers:
"You're trembling."

The skyscrapers told the street vendors:
"Close up. Rains are coming."

The vendors told the air:
"Our sleeves are filling with your wind."

The air told all the bridges:
"You're agitating, and the water reflects you."

The bridges told the river:
"Don't leave us."

Night Walks

1.

I don't know where I live,
                    happy in my blur of work,
a walk around town, talk,
scribbling, a good two hours of reading
in a cafe chair; I love
                    being enclosed in fair weather,
early February, when the sky is wired & lucid over the city,
and the dark blues stay blue
till 6:30 when the web of lights
casts orange nets over the rivers.
                            I don't know
a name for this shade of gold—
                    buttery but with roses in it—
like my favorite gold coin necklace,
                    Ceres' face on it,
full & round, strong nose, prominent chin,
gold beads at her throat. And the tangle of her hair?
Wheat & stars, loops, weaves,
the bodies of dolphins, twists & knots
of hair, oak leaves, plumes,
the broad forehead.
                    Am I describing Earth, will I ever
fathom the ropes & fawns of her oiled, close-to-the-scalp
head of hair, heavy browbone
& thick lid over the round eye?
Her thick neck scented with
                    the beginnings of everything—
                        mother—
and the end of nothing,
Ceres' earring's inverted V, little shovel,
another emblem of vulva
                  where the end of everything
meets the beginning of everything.

2.

Tonight I feel like a lucky coin
far from the fields where no one walks:
East of the city I open my eyes, Tu Fu said.
But out there, out where the edge of the city thins away,
                        old trees sag & bend,
sumac & locust call to me
to walk off into folds of snow
hemming the tree trunks
                  where horses stand near graves—
                        my oldest dead—

Out there the willows
whose branches are thin as gypsy whips
rasp the old town's name: Rzeszow, beloved Carpathian village
of the old little mothers:

like a whip
like my mother's name: Gunia/horsehair.
Just off the village square
one *gestapo* follows my mother's mother
who has stepped out of her kitchen
to smoke a cigar, then stand in line for bread.
He eyes her like a camera
                though no pictures of that time
were made. Just off the square

my melancholy began, there,
               in a kitchen three steps from the street,
carrots & potatoes   chopped   soaked   boiled   braised
in the oiled black skillet
dressed with snipped chives & yellow onions. O
the afternoon is so long & grey.
                The sour smell is her sweat
& a cut lemon & the stale paste of false teeth breath.
I trip over the sound of the knife
against the cutting board,
             I trip over her feet

her brooms, her brushes.
                                   I listened to my mother reading letters
to her mother & all the other old ones
while I breathed inside her belly.
That's how I learned to listen
to a kitchen, a street.
                         My idea of hell is that kitchen
where the women worked all day and did not sit down to eat
until they had served the men,
and the men had eaten & drunk,

            but out here
            my mind clears, my body emerges
            to take the shape of space
            the walk gives it.
                  Wary Proserpine, I'm
                     in awe of the blue roads, here,

at the edge of my city
winding me back in.
Flanks of our ancient hills
wear hundreds of shades of brown & gray.
The roads coil & uncoil
over our wide basins,
our waterways & inlets,
the channels
now feeble, now flooded.
The brooklets & gutters run hard
after this morning's heavy summer storm.
The form of a city changes faster than the heart of a mortal.

3.

Melancholy's like reading Rilke:
being slowly & sweetly poisoned to death,
                                   death by IV from the stars,
by way of the sky's open vault.
Moody night, you have something to do
                              with rage,
with houselessness,
                  though I have a house

tight as a ship &
with as many leaks & hiding places.
I gave up on Rilke when I decided
                              I'm still not old enough
to read him. I walk.
                    Up the avenues & through parking lots
& bus stops where it gets hazy & backlit after 12.

                         There's only one human that I know of
sleeping on cardboard near the Carnegie.
The vents are broad there
and the foyers of the University
are generously dark.
I'm taking the side streets now,
                    I'm under the lights
and can be seen & safe.
                    Down by the rivers there are more
under bridges, sleeping against the bulwarks.
                    In season, Proserpine will join them.

There is no consciousness anymore except in the streets
because there is history only in the streets,
so runs the decree, Camus said.
                    He was sad,
hungry for the sea, hills, evening meditations.
                              All my teachers
have given me the same gift:
writing is a walk,
never the same twice.
                    Someone from the city paper
tried living under the bridges and reporting about it
but he was attacked
in print
          because he could go home to his apartment
every night if he wanted to, after all.
That is privilege.

But I say make use of it.
If you can't sleep, get up.